PUBLICATIONS INTERNATIONAL, LTD.

Photography: Sanders Studios, Inc.
Photographer: Kathy Sanders
Prop Stylist: Christine Nestor
Studio Coordinator: Kathy Ores
Food Stylists: Teri Rys-Maki, Diane Hugh
Assistant Food Stylist: Laura Bednarski

Pictured on the front cover *(clockwise from top left):* Festive Easter Cookies *(page 50),* Chocolate Teddy Bears *(page 22),* Handprint *(page 20),* Rainbows *(page 28)* and Critters-in-Holes *(page 26).*

Pictured on the back cover *(top to bottom):* Gingerbread Farm Animals in Corral *(page 34),* Sunshine Butter Cookie *(page 42)* and Chocolate Pinwheels *(page 44).*

ISBN: 0-7853-2846-7

Manufactured in U.S.A.

8 7 6 5 4 3 2 1

Microwave Cooking: Microwave ovens vary in wattage. Use the cooking times as guidelines and check for doneness before adding more time.

Crazy for Cookie Dough

Flip through the pages of this delightful book and see all the wonderful ways to use cookie dough. Set aside some time, perhaps the next rainy day to do projects with your family. Use the suggestions and photos as a starting point and let your imagination go wild! Feel free to change the colors or shapes to suit your family or party.

General Guidelines

• Measure all the ingredients and assemble them in the order called for in the recipe.

• All cookie dough should be well chilled before using. Unless the recipe states otherwise, work with the recommended portion of dough called for and refrigerate the remaining dough until needed.

• Follow recipe directions and baking times. Check for doneness using the test given in the recipe.

• Most refrigerated cookie dough expands considerably when baked. Always leave two inches between cookies when placing them on cookie sheets.

Supplies:

Some of the recipes in *Cookie Dough Fun* call for special equipment or nonfood items; these are always listed in the recipe under the heading "Supplies." Most of the supplies listed are available in stores carrying cake decorating equipment and in supermarkets.

Kitchen Equipment:

Equipment not listed under "Supplies" are things that are normally found in a well-equipped kitchen including: mixing bowls, cookie and baking sheets, rolling pins, small, medium and large saucepans, aluminum foil, waxed paper and cookie cutters.

Additional equipment you may need that is listed under "Supplies" includes: pastry brush, lollipop sticks, cardboard, pastry bags and decorating tips.

Special Techniques

Making Patterns:

When a pattern is to be used only once, make the pattern out of waxed paper. Using the diagram(s) and photo as guides, draw the pattern pieces on waxed paper. Cut the pieces out and place them on the rolled-out dough. Cut around the pattern pieces with a sharp knife. Remove the pattern pieces and discard. Continue as directed in the recipe.

For patterns that are used more than once, make the pattern more durable by using clean lightweight cardboard or poster board. Using the diagram(s) and photo as guides, draw the pattern pieces on the cardboard. Cut the pieces out and lightly spray one side with nonstick cooking spray. Place the pattern pieces, sprayed side down, on the rolled-out dough and cut around them with a sharp knife. Reuse the pattern pieces to make as many cutouts as needed.

Tinting Coconut:

Dilute a few drops of food color with ½ teaspoon water in a large plastic food storage bag. Add 1 to 1⅓ cups flaked coconut. Close the bag and shake well until the coconut is evenly coated. If a deeper color is desired, add more diluted food color and shake again.

Melting Chocolate:

When melting chocolate be sure the utensils are completely dry. Any drop of moisture makes the chocolate become stiff and grainy. If this does happen, add ½ teaspoon shortening (not butter) for each ounce of chocolate and stir until smooth. Chocolate scorches easily, and once scorched cannot be used. Use one of the following three methods for successful melting.

Double Boiler: Place the chocolate in the top of a double boiler or in a heatproof bowl over hot, not boiling water. Stir until smooth. (Make sure the water remains just below a simmer and is one inch below the top pan.) Be careful that no steam or water gets into the chocolate.

Direct Heat: Place the chocolate in a heavy saucepan and melt over very low heat, stirring constantly. Remove the chocolate from the heat as soon as it is melted. Be sure to watch the chocolate carefully since it is easily scorched with this method.

Microwave Oven: Place a 1-ounce square of chocolate or 1 cup of chocolate chips in a small microwavable bowl. Microwave at HIGH 1 to 2 minutes or until the chocolate is almost melted, stirring well after every minute. Add 10 seconds for each additional ounce of chocolate. Be sure to stir the microwaved chocolate well because it retains its original shape even when melted.

"Everything but the Kitchen Sink" Bar Cookies

What you need:

1 package
    (18 ounces)
    refrigerated
    chocolate chip
    cookie dough
1 jar (7 ounces)
    marshmallow
    creme
½ cup creamy peanut
    butter
1½ cups toasted corn
    cereal
½ cup miniature
    candy-coated
    chocolate pieces

1 Preheat oven to 350°F. Grease 13×9-inch baking pan. Remove dough from wrapper according to package directions.

2 Press dough into prepared baking pan. Bake 13 minutes.

3 Remove baking pan from oven. Drop teaspoonfuls of marshmallow creme and peanut butter over hot cookie base.

4 Bake 1 minute. Carefully spread marshmallow creme and peanut butter over cookie base.

5 Sprinkle cereal and chocolate pieces over melted marshmallow and peanut butter mixture.

6 Bake 7 minutes. Cool completely on wire rack. Cut into 2-inch bars.
    Makes 3 dozen bar cookies

"Everything but the Kitchen
Sink" Bar Cookies

Sandwich Cookies

What you need:

**1 package (20 ounces)
refrigerated cookie
dough, any flavor
All-purpose flour
(optional)**

FILLINGS

**Any combination of
colored frostings,
peanut butter or
assorted ice creams**

DECORATIONS

**Colored sprinkles,
chocolate-covered
raisins, miniature
candy-coated
chocolate pieces
and other assorted
small candies**

1 Preheat oven to 350°F.
Grease cookie sheets.

2 Remove dough from
wrapper according to
package directions.

3 Cut dough into 4 equal
sections. Reserve
1 section; refrigerate remaining
3 sections.

4 Roll reserved dough to
¼-inch thickness. Sprinkle
with flour to minimize sticking, if
necessary.

5 Cut out cookies using
1 (¾-inch) round cookie
cutter. Transfer cookies to
prepared cookie sheets, placing
about 2 inches apart. Repeat
steps with remaining dough.

6 Bake 8 to 11 minutes or
until edges are lightly
browned. Remove to wire racks;
cool completely.

7 To make sandwich, spread
about 1 tablespoon desired
filling to within ¼ inch of the
underside of 1 cookie. Top with
second cookie, pressing gently.

8 Roll side of sandwich in
desired decorations.
Repeat with remaining cookies.
*Makes about 20 to 24 sandwich
cookies*

Tip

*Be creative—make sandwich
cookies using 2 or more flavors of
refrigerated cookie dough. Mix
and match to see how many flavor
combinations you can come up
with.*

Peanuts

What you need:

½ **cup butter or margarine, softened**
¼ **cup shortening**
¼ **cup creamy peanut butter**
1 **cup powdered sugar, sifted**
1 **egg yolk**
1 **teaspoon vanilla**
1¾ **cups all-purpose flour**
1 **cup finely ground honey-roasted peanuts, divided**
Peanut Buttery Frosting (recipe follows)

1 Grease cookie sheets.

2 Beat butter, shortening and peanut butter in large bowl at medium speed of electric mixer. Gradually add powdered sugar, beating until smooth. Add egg yolk and vanilla; beat well. Add flour; mix well. Stir in ⅓ cup ground peanuts. Cover dough; refrigerate 1 hour.

3 Prepare Peanut Buttery Frosting. Preheat oven to 350°F. Shape dough into 1-inch balls. Place 2 balls, side by side and slightly touching, on prepared cookie sheet. Gently flatten balls with fingertips and form into "peanut" shape. Repeat steps with remaining dough.

4 Bake 16 to 18 minutes or until edges are lightly browned. Cool on cookie sheets 5 minutes. Remove cookies to wire racks; cool completely.

5 Place remaining ⅔ cup ground peanuts in shallow dish. Spread about 2 teaspoons Peanut Buttery Frosting evenly over top of each cookie. Coat with ground peanuts.
Makes about 2 dozen cookies

Peanut Buttery Frosting

½ **cup butter or margarine, softened**
½ **cup creamy peanut butter**
2 **cups powdered sugar, sifted**
½ **teaspoon vanilla**
3 **to 6 tablespoons milk**

1 Beat butter and peanut butter in medium bowl at medium speed of electric mixer until smooth. Gradually add powdered sugar and vanilla until blended but crumbly.

2 Add milk, 1 tablespoon at a time, until smooth. Refrigerate until ready to use.
Makes 1⅓ cups frosting

Butter Pretzel Cookies

What you need:

1 recipe Butter Cookie Dough (page 61)

TOPPINGS

White, rainbow or colored rock or coarse sugar

1 Prepare Butter Cookie Dough. Cover; refrigerate about 4 hours or until firm.

2 Preheat oven to 350°F. Grease cookie sheets.

3 Divide dough into 4 equal sections. Reserve 1 section; refrigerate remaining 3 sections. Divide reserved dough into 4 equal pieces. Roll each dough piece on lightly floured surface to 12-inch rope; sprinkle with rock or coarse sugar.

4 Transfer 1 rope at a time to prepared cookie sheets. Form each rope into pretzel shape. Repeat steps with remaining dough pieces.

5 Bake 14 to 18 minutes or until edges begin to brown. Cool cookies on cookie sheets 1 minute. Remove to wire racks; cool completely.

Makes 16 cookies

Chocolate Pretzel Cookies

What you need:

1 recipe Chocolate Cookie Dough (page 61)

TOPPINGS

White and colored rock or coarse sugar

1 Prepare Chocolate Cookie Dough. Cover; refrigerate about 2 hours or until firm.

2 Preheat oven to 325°F. Grease cookie sheets.

3 Divide dough into 4 equal sections. Reserve 1 section; refrigerate remaining 3 sections. Divide reserved dough into 5 equal pieces. Roll each dough piece on lightly floured surface to 12-inch rope; sprinkle with rock or coarse sugar.

4 Transfer 1 rope at a time to prepared cookie sheets. Form each rope into pretzel shape. Repeat steps with remaining dough pieces.

5 Bake 12 to 14 minutes or until edges begin to brown. Cool cookies on cookie sheets 1 minute. Remove to wire racks; cool completely.

Makes 20 cookies

Butter Pretzel Cookies, Chocolate Pretzel Cookies

Peanut Butter and Chocolate Spirals

What you need:

1 package (20 ounces) refrigerated sugar cookie dough
1 package (20 ounces) refrigerated peanut butter cookie dough
¼ cup unsweetened cocoa powder
⅓ cup peanut butter-flavored chips, chopped
¼ cup all-purpose flour
⅓ cup miniature chocolate chips

1 Remove each dough from wrapper according to package directions.

2 Place sugar cookie dough and cocoa in large bowl; mix with fork to blend. Stir in peanut butter chips.

3 Place peanut butter cookie dough and flour in another large bowl; mix with fork to blend. Stir in chocolate chips. Divide each dough in half; refrigerate 1 hour.

4 Roll each dough on floured surface to 6×12-inch rectangle. Layer each half of peanut butter dough onto each half of chocolate dough. Roll up dough, starting at long end to form 2 (12-inch) rolls. Refrigerate 1 hour.

5 Preheat oven to 375°F. Cut dough into ½-inch-thick slices. Place cookies 2 inches apart on ungreased cookie sheets.

6 Bake 10 to 12 minutes or until lightly browned. Remove to wire racks; cool completely.

Makes 4 dozen cookies

Kids' Cookie Dough

What you need:

1 cup butter, softened
2 teaspoons vanilla
½ cup powdered sugar
2¼ cups all-purpose
flour
¼ teaspoon salt

DECORATIONS
Assorted colored
glazes, frostings,
sugars and small
candies

1 Preheat oven to 350°F. Grease cookie sheets.

2 Beat butter and vanilla in large bowl at high speed of electric mixer until fluffy. Add sugar and beat at medium speed until blended.

3 Combine flour and salt in small bowl. Gradually add to butter mixture.

4 Divide dough into 10 equal sections. Form shapes directly on prepared cookie sheets according to photo, or as desired, for each section.

5 Bake 15 to 18 minutes or until edges are lightly browned. Cool completely on cookie sheets.

6 Decorate with glazes, frostings, sugars and small candies as desired.
Makes 10 (4-inch) cookies

Kids' Cookie Dough

Cookie Canvases

What you need:

1 package (20 ounces)
refrigerated cookie
dough, any flavor
All-purpose flour
(optional)
1 recipe Cookie Glaze
(page 62)

SUPPLIES
1 (3½-inch) square
cardboard template
1 (2½×4½-inch)
rectangular
cardboard template
Assorted liquid food
colors
Small craft paint
brushes

1 Preheat oven to 350°F.
Grease cookie sheets.

2 Remove dough from
wrapper according to
package directions. Cut dough
in half. Wrap half of dough in
plastic wrap and refrigerate.

3 Roll remaining dough on
floured surface to ¼-inch
thickness. Sprinkle with flour to
minimize sticking, if necessary.
Cut out cookie shapes using
cardboard templates as guides.
Place cookies 2 inches apart on
prepared cookie sheets. Repeat
steps with remaining dough.

4 Bake 8 to 10 minutes or
until edges are lightly
browned. Remove from oven
and straighten cookie edges
with spatula. Cool cookies
completely on cookie sheets.
Prepare Cookie Glaze.

5 Place cookies on wire
racks set over waxed paper.
Drizzle Cookie Glaze over
cookies. Let stand at room
temperature 40 minutes or until
glaze is set. Place food colors in
small bowls. Using small craft
paint brushes, decorate cookies
with food colors by "painting"
designs such as rainbows,
flowers and animals.
Makes 8 to 10 cookie canvases

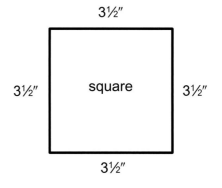

3½″ · square · 3½″ (3½″ top, 3½″ bottom)

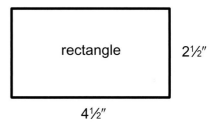

rectangle · 2½″ · 4½″

Handprints

What you need:

**1 package (20 ounces) refrigerated cookie dough, any flavor
All-purpose flour (optional)**

DECORATIONS

Cookie glazes, frostings, nondairy whipped topping, peanut butter and assorted candies

1 Grease cookie sheets.

2 Remove dough from wrapper according to package directions.

3 Cut dough into 4 equal sections. Reserve 1 section; refrigerate remaining 3 sections. Sprinkle reserved dough with flour to minimize sticking, if necessary.

4 Roll dough on prepared cookie sheet to 5×7-inch rectangle.

5 Place hand, palm-side down, on dough. Carefully, cut around outline of hand with knife. Remove scraps. Separate fingers as much as possible using small spatula. Pat fingers outward to lengthen slightly. Repeat steps with remaining dough.

6 Freeze dough 15 minutes. Preheat oven to 350°F.

7 Bake 7 to 13 minutes or until cookies are set and edges are golden brown. Cool completely on cookie sheets.

8 Decorate as desired.
Makes 5 adult handprint cookies

Tip

To get the kids involved, let them use their hands to make the handprints. Be sure that an adult is available to cut around the outline with a knife. The kids will enjoy seeing how their handprints bake into big cookies.

Chocolate Teddy Bears

What you need:

1 recipe Chocolate Cookie Dough (page 61)

DECORATIONS
White and colored frostings, decorator gels, coarse sugars and assorted small candies

1 Prepare Chocolate Cookie Dough. Cover; refrigerate about 2 hours or until firm.

2 Preheat oven to 325°F. Grease cookie sheets.

3 Divide dough in half. Reserve 1 half; refrigerate remaining dough.

4 Divide reserved dough into 8 equal balls. Cut 1 ball in half; roll 1 half into ball for body.

5 Cut other half into 2 equal pieces; roll 1 piece into 4 small balls for paws.

6 Divide second piece into thirds. Roll two-thirds of dough into ball for head.

7 Divide remaining one-third of dough in half; roll into 2 small balls for ears.

8 Place balls together directly on prepared cookie sheet to form bear according to diagram. Repeat steps with remaining dough.

9 Bake 13 to 15 minutes or until set. Cool completely on cookie sheets. Decorate with frostings, gels, sugars and assorted candies as desired.
Makes 16 (4-inch) teddy bears

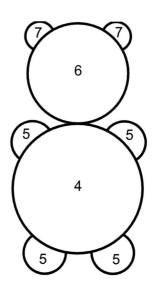

Numbers in diagram refer to steps in recipe.

Chocolate Teddy Bears

Puzzle Cookie

What you need:

¾ cup shortening
½ cup packed light
    brown sugar
6 tablespoons dark
    molasses
2 egg whites
¾ teaspoon vanilla
2¼ cups all-purpose flour
¾ teaspoon baking soda
¼ teaspoon plus
    ⅛ teaspoon baking
    powder
¾ teaspoon salt
2 teaspoons ground
    cinnamon
¾ teaspoon ground
    ginger

DECORATIONS

Assorted colored
    frostings, colored
    sugars, colored
    decorator gels and
    assorted small
    candies

1 Beat shortening, brown sugar, molasses, egg whites and vanilla in large bowl at high speed of electric mixer until smooth.

2 Combine flour, baking soda, baking powder, salt, cinnamon and ginger in medium bowl. Add to shortening mixture; mix well. Shape dough into flat rectangle. Wrap in plastic wrap and refrigerate about 8 hours or until firm.

3 Preheat oven to 350°F. Grease jelly-roll pan.

4 Sprinkle dough with additional flour. Place dough in center of prepared pan and roll evenly to within ½ inch of edge of pan. Cut shapes into dough according to photo, using cookie cutters or free-hand, allowing at least 1 inch between each shape. Cut through dough using sharp knife, but do not remove cookie shapes.

5 Bake 12 minutes or until edges begin to brown lightly. Remove from oven and retrace shapes with knife. Return to oven 5 to 6 minutes. Cool in pan 5 minutes. Carefully remove shapes to wire racks; cool completely.

6 Decorate shapes with frostings, sugars, decorator gels and small candies as shown in photo. Leave puzzle frame in pan. Decorate with frostings, colored sugars and gels to represent sky, clouds, grass and water, if desired. Return shapes to their respective openings to complete puzzle.

Makes 1 (15×10-inch) puzzle cookie

Critters-in-Holes

What you need:

48 **chewy caramel candies coated in milk chocolate**
48 **pieces candy corn**
Miniature candy-coated chocolate pieces
1 **container frosting, any flavor**
1 **package (20 ounces) refrigerated peanut butter cookie dough**

1 Cut slit into side of 1 caramel candy using sharp knife.

2 Carefully insert 1 piece candy corn into slit. Repeat with remaining caramel candies and candy corn.

3 Attach miniature chocolate pieces to caramel candies to resemble "eyes" using frosting as glue. Decorate as desired.

4 Preheat oven to 350°F. Grease 12 (1¾-inch) muffin cups.

5 Remove dough from wrapper according to package directions. Cut dough into 12 (1-inch) slices. Cut each slice into 4 equal sections. Place 1 section of dough into each muffin cup.

6 Bake 9 minutes. Remove from oven and immediately press 1 decorated caramel candy into center of each cookie. Repeat with remaining ingredients.

7 Remove to wire racks; cool completely.
Makes 4 dozen cookies

Rainbows

What you need:

**1 recipe Christmas
Ornament Cookie
Dough (page 62)
Red, green, yellow and
blue paste food
colors**

DECORATIONS
**White frosting and
gold glitter dust**

1 Prepare Christmas
Ornament Cookie Dough.
Divide dough into 10 equal
sections. Combine 4 sections
dough and red food coloring in
large bowl; blend until smooth.

2 Combine 3 sections dough
and green food coloring in
medium bowl; blend until
smooth.

3 Combine 2 sections dough
and yellow food coloring in
another medium bowl; blend
until smooth.

4 Combine remaining dough
and blue food coloring in
small bowl; blend until smooth.
Wrap each section of dough in
plastic wrap. Refrigerate
30 minutes.

5 Shape blue dough into
8-inch log. Shape yellow
dough into 8×3-inch rectangle;
place on waxed paper. Place
blue log in center of yellow

rectangle. Fold yellow edges up
and around blue log, pinching to
seal. Roll to form smooth log.

6 Roll green dough into 8×5-
inch rectangle on waxed
paper. Place yellow log in center
of green rectangle. Fold green
edges up and around yellow log.
Pinch to seal. Roll gently to form
smooth log.

7 Roll red dough into 8×7-
inch rectangle. Place green
log in center of red rectangle.
Fold red edges up and around
green log. Pinch to seal. Roll
gently to form smooth log. Wrap
in plastic wrap. Refrigerate
1 hour.

8 Preheat oven to 350°F.
Grease cookie sheets. Cut
log in half lengthwise. Cut each
half into ¼-inch-thick slices.
Place slices 1 inch apart on
prepared cookie sheets. Bake
8 to 12 minutes. (Do not brown.)
Cool on cookie sheets 1 minute.
Remove to wire racks; cool
completely.

9 Pipe small amount of
frosting on bottom corner of
1 side of each cookie and
sprinkle with glitter dust. Let
stand 1 hour or until frosting
sets.

Makes about 5 dozen cookies

Domino Cookies

What you need:

**1 package (20 ounces) refrigerated sugar cookie dough
All-purpose flour (optional)
½ cup semisweet chocolate chips**

1 Preheat oven to 350°F. Grease cookie sheets.

2 Remove dough from wrapper according to package directions. Cut dough into 4 equal sections. Reserve 1 section; refrigerate remaining 3 sections.

3 Roll reserved dough to ⅛-inch thickness. Sprinkle with flour to minimize sticking, if necessary.

4 Cut out 9 (1¾×2½-inch) rectangles according to diagram using sharp knife. Place 2 inches apart on prepared cookies sheets.

5 Score each cookie across middle with sharp knife.

6 Gently press chocolate chips, point side down, into dough to resemble various dominos. Repeat with remaining dough and scraps.

 7 Bake 8 to 10 minutes or until edges are light golden brown. Remove to wire racks; cool completely.

Makes 36 cookies

────────(Tip)────────

Use these adorable cookies as a learning tool for kids. They can count the number of chocolate chips in each cookie and arrange them in lots of ways: highest to lowest, numerically or even solve simple math problems. As a treat, they can eat the cookies afterwards.

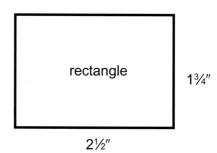

rectangle

1¾"

2½"

Hot Dog Cookies

What you need:

**1 recipe Butter Cookie
Dough (page 61)
Liquid food colors
Sesame seeds**

**TOPPINGS
Shredded coconut, red
and green decorator
gels, frosting and
gummy candies**

1 Prepare Butter Cookie
Dough. Cover; refrigerate
4 hours or until firm. Grease
cookie sheets.

2 Use ⅓ of dough to make
"hot dogs." Refrigerate
remaining dough. Mix food
colors in small bowl to get
reddish-brown color following
chart on back of food color box.
Add reserved ⅓ of dough. Mix
color throughout dough using
wooden spoon.

3 Divide colored dough into
6 equal sections. Roll each
section into thin log shape.
Round edges. Set aside.

4 To make "buns," divide
remaining dough into
6 equal sections.

5 Roll sections into thick logs.
Make very deep indentation
the length of log in centers;
smooth edges to create buns.

6 Lift buns with small spatula
and dip sides in sesame
seeds. Place 3 inches apart on
prepared cookie sheets.

7 Place hot dogs inside buns.

8 Freeze 20 minutes. Preheat
oven to 350°F. Bake 17 to
20 minutes or until bun edges
are light golden brown. Cool
completely on cookie sheets.

9 Top hot dogs with green-
tinted shredded coconut for
"relish," white coconut for
"onions," red decorator gel for
"ketchup" and yellow-tinted
frosting or whipped topping for
"mustard."

Makes 6 hot dog cookies

 Tip

*To pipe gels and frosting onto Hot
Dog Cookies, you can use a
resealable plastic sandwich bag
as a substitute for a pastry bag.
Fold the top of the bag down to
form a cuff and use a spatula to
fill bag half full with gel or
frosting. Unfold top of bag and
twist down against filling. Snip tiny
tip off one corner of bag. Hold
top of bag tightly and squeeze
filling through opening.*

Gingerbread Farm Animals in Corral

What you need:

**1 recipe Gingerbread
Construction Dough
(page 62)
2 recipes Royal Icing
(page 61)**

DECORATIONS

**Assorted food colors
Shredded coconut
Assorted small hard
candies**

SUPPLIES

**Cardboard
Decorative paper**

1 Preheat oven to 375°F.
Prepare Gingerbread
Construction Dough. Divide
dough into 4 equal sections. To
make fence, roll 1 section of
dough directly onto large cookie
sheet to ¼-inch thickness. Cut
into 6 (2¾×6-inch) sections,
leaving ½-inch space between
sections. Bake 10 to 12 minutes
or until edges are browned.
Cool completely on wire racks.

2 Roll second section of
dough directly onto cookie
sheet to ¼-inch thickness. Cut
into 4 (2¾×6-inch) sections and
2 (3-inch) sections. Bake 10 to
12 minutes or until edges are
browned. Cool completely on
wire racks.

3 To make animals, roll
remaining 2 sections of
dough directly on cookie sheets
to ⅛-inch thickness. Cut out
animal shapes using animal-
shaped cookie cutters. Bake
8 to 12 minutes or until edges
are browned. Cool completely
on wire racks.

4 Prepare Royal Icing. Tint
small amounts of icing with
food colors to decorate animals.
Place remaining icing in small
resealable plastic food storage
bag. Cut off small corner of bag
for piping.

5 Decorate animals and
fence sections with icing
and assorted candies according
to photo. Cover 20-inch piece of
cardboard with decorative paper
and plastic wrap. Assemble
fence by piping icing on bottom
and side edges of fence
sections. Use smaller sections
to make 2 gates. Pipe icing on
feet of animals; arrange so
animals can be supported by
fence or other animals. Sprinkle
green-tinted coconut around
feet of animals for grass, if
desired.

*Makes 1 fence and 2 dozen
animals*

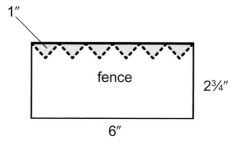

**Gingerbread Farm Animals in
Corral**

Shapers

What you need:

2 packages (20 ounces each) refrigerated sugar cookie dough
Red, yellow, green and blue paste food colors

DECORATIONS
1 container vanilla frosting

1 Remove dough from wrapper according to package directions. Cut each roll of dough in half.

2 Beat ¼ of dough and red food coloring in medium bowl at medium speed of electric mixer until well blended.

3 Roll red dough on sheet of waxed paper to 5-inch log. Set aside.

4 Repeat with remaining dough and food colors. Cover; refrigerate tinted logs 1 hour or until firm.

5 Working with one log at a time, roll on smooth surface to create circular, triangular, square and oval shaped logs. Use ruler to keep triangle and square sides flat.

6 Cover; refrigerate dough 1 hour or until firm.

7 Preheat oven to 350°F. Cut shaped dough into ¼-inch slices. Place 2 inches apart on ungreased baking sheets.

8 Bake 9 to 12 minutes. Remove to wire racks; cool completely.

9 Spoon frosting into resealable plastic food storage bag; seal. Cut tiny tip from corner of bag.

10 Pipe frosting around each cookie to define shape.
Makes about 6½ dozen cookies

 Tip

If you have extra liquid food colors at home, tint the vanilla frosting different colors. Frost cookies using contrasting colored frosting, for example green frosting on a red cookie.

Cookie Pops

What you need:

**1 package
(20 ounces)
refrigerated sugar
cookie dough
All-purpose flour
(optional)**

**SUPPLIES
20 (4-inch) lollipop
sticks**

**DECORATIONS
Assorted colored
sugars, frostings,
glazes and gels**

1 Preheat oven to 350°F. Grease cookie sheets.

2 Remove dough from wrapper according to package directions.

3 Sprinkle with flour to minimize sticking, if necessary. Cut dough in half.

Reserve 1 half; refrigerate remaining dough.

4 Roll reserved dough to ⅛-inch thickness. Cut out cookies using 3½-inch cookie cutters.

5 Place lollipop sticks on cookies so that tips of sticks are imbedded in cookies. Carefully turn cookies so sticks are in back; place on prepared cookie sheets. Repeat with remaining dough.

6 Bake 7 to 11 minutes or until edges are lightly browned. Cool cookies on cookie sheets 2 minutes. Remove cookies to wire racks; cool completely.

7 Decorate with colored sugars, frostings, glazes and gels as desired.
Makes 20 cookies

Cookie Pops

KATE

FRANK

Name Jewelry

What you need:

1 recipe Christmas Ornament Cookie Dough (page 62)

SUPPLIES
Plastic drinking straw
Thin ribbon or yarn

DECORATIONS
White Icing (recipe follows)
Colored sugars
Assorted food colors (optional)
Small candies (optional)

1 Prepare Christmas Ornament Cookie Dough. Divide dough in half; wrap in plastic wrap. Refrigerate 30 minutes or until firm.

2 Preheat oven to 350°F. Grease cookie sheets.

3 Roll ½ of dough on floured surface to ¼-inch thickness. Cut out cookies using 3¾-inch cookie cutters of various shapes, such as rectangles, circles and hearts.

4 Place cookies on prepared cookie sheets. With plastic straw, make holes in tops of cookies, about ½ inch from top edges.

5 Bake 10 to 12 minutes or until edges begin to brown. Remove cookies to wire racks; cool completely. If necessary, push straw through warm cookies to remake holes.

6 Cut ribbon into 18 (32-inch) pieces. Thread ribbon through holes.

7 Prepare White Icing; spread over cookies. Let stand 40 minutes or until set. Spoon colored or additional icing into small resealable plastic food storage bag. Cut tiny tip from corner of bag. Pipe individual names directly onto cookies as shown in photo. Let stand until set. Decorate with colored sugars and small candies, if desired.

Makes about 18 cookie necklaces

White Icing

2 cups powdered sugar
2 tablespoons milk or lemon juice

Combine powdered sugar and milk in small bowl until smooth. (Icing will be very thick. Stir in 1 teaspoon additional milk, if desired.) Icing may be divided into small bowls and tinted with food coloring, if desired.

Sunshine Butter Cookies

What you need:

¾ cup butter, softened
¾ cup sugar
1 egg
2¼ cups all-purpose flour
¼ teaspoon salt
    Grated peel of
      ½ lemon
1 teaspoon frozen
    lemonade
    concentrate, thawed
1 recipe Lemonade
    Royal Icing (page 61)
1 egg, beaten
    Thin pretzel sticks
    Yellow paste food
    color

DECORATIONS

    Gummy fruit and black
    licorice strings

1 Beat butter and sugar in large bowl at high speed of electric mixer until fluffy. Add egg; beat well.

2 Combine flour, salt and lemon peel in medium bowl. Add to butter mixture. Stir in lemonade concentrate. Refrigerate 2 hours.

3 Prepare Lemonade Royal Icing. Cover; let stand at room temperature. Preheat oven to 350°F. Grease cookie sheets.

4 Roll dough on floured surface to ⅛-inch thickness. Cut out cookies using 3-inch round cookie cutter. Place cookies on prepared cookie sheets. Brush cookies with beaten egg. Arrange pretzel sticks around edge of cookies to resemble sunshine rays; press gently. Bake 10 minutes or until lightly browned. Remove to wire racks; cool completely.

5 Add food color to Lemonade Royal Icing. Spoon about ½ cup icing into resealable plastic food storage bag; seal. Cut tiny tip from corner of bag. Pipe thin circle around underside of each cookie to create outline.

6 Add water, 1 tablespoon at a time, to remaining icing in bowl, until thick but pourable consistency. Spoon icing in cookie centers staying within outline.

7 Decorate cookies with fruit snacks and licorice as shown in photo. Let stand 1 hour or until dry.
Makes about 3 dozen cookies

Chocolate Pinwheels

What you need:

1 recipe Chocolate Cookie Dough (page 61)

SUPPLIES
24 wooden popsicle sticks

DECORATIONS
24 (¼-inch) round hard candies or other candies
Assorted colored sugars

1 Prepare Chocolate Cookie Dough. Cover; refrigerate 1 hour or until firm.

2 Preheat oven to 325°F. Grease cookie sheets. Place popsicle sticks 4 inches apart on prepared cookie sheets.

3 Roll dough on floured surface to ¼-inch thickness. Cut out cookies using 3-inch round cookie cutter.

4 Place 1 dough round on end of each wooden stick, pressing down. Cut 4 (1-inch) slits around the edge of each dough round according to diagram.

5 Lift 1 side of each slit, bringing the corner to the center of the cookie and pressing gently. Repeat with remaining dough. Place round candy in center of each pinwheel cookie.

6 Bake 10 minutes or until set. Remove to wire racks; cool completely. Decorate with colored sugars.
Makes 2 dozen cookies

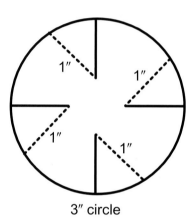

1" 1" 1" 1"

3" circle

Chocolate Pinwheels

Letters of the Alphabet

What you need:

1 recipe Gingerbread Cookie Dough (page 60)

DECORATIONS

Colored frostings and glazes, colored sugars, sprinkles and assorted small candies

1 Prepare Gingerbread Cookie Dough. Cover; refrigerate about 8 hours or until firm.

2 Preheat oven to 350°F. Grease cookie sheets.

3 Divide dough into 4 equal sections. Reserve 1 section; refrigerate remaining 3 sections.

4 Roll reserved dough on floured surface to ⅛-inch thickness. Sprinkle with flour to minimize sticking, if necessary.

5 Transfer dough to 1 corner of prepared cookie sheet.

6 Cut out alphabet letter shapes using 2½-inch cookie cutters. Repeat steps with remaining dough.

7 Bake 6 to 8 minutes or until edges begin to brown. Remove cookies to wire racks; cool completely.

8 Decorate cookies with frostings, glazes, colored sugars, sprinkles and assorted small candies.

Makes about 5 dozen cookies

Tip

Encourage children to arrange letters to spell names of people they know, their favorite animals or pets, colors or even places they like to go. A tasty way to learn the ABC's.

YOU'RE INVITED TO A PARTY

Cookie Cups

What you need:

**1 package (20 ounces) refrigerated sugar cookie dough
All-purpose flour (optional)**

**FILLINGS
Prepared pudding, nondairy whipped topping, maraschino cherries, jelly beans, assorted sprinkles and small candies**

1 Grease 12 (2¾-inch) muffin cups.

2 Remove dough from wrapper according to package directions. Sprinkle dough with flour to minimize sticking, if necessary.

3 Cut dough into 12 equal pieces; roll into balls. Place 1 ball in bottom of each muffin cup. Press dough halfway up sides of muffin cup, making indentation in center of dough.

4 Freeze muffin cups 15 minutes. Preheat oven to 350°F.

5 Bake 15 to 17 minutes or until golden brown. Cookies will be puffy. Remove from oven; gently press indentation with teaspoon.

6 Return to oven 1 to 2 minutes. Cool cookies in muffin cups 5 minutes. Remove to wire racks; cool completely.

7 Fill each cookie cup with desired fillings. Decorate as desired.

Makes 12 cookie cups

Giant Cookie Cups Variation: Grease 10 (3¾-inch) muffin cups. Cut dough into 10 pieces; roll into balls. Complete recipe according to regular Cookie Cup directions. Makes 10 giant cookie cups.

Tip

Add some pizzazz to your cookie cups by filling with a mixture of prepared fruit-flavored gelatin combined with prepared pudding or nondairy whipped topping. For convenience, snack-size gelatins and puddings can be found at the supermarket, so there is no need to make them from scratch.

JUST
FOR
YOU

Festive Easter Cookies

What you need:

1 cup butter or margarine, softened
2 cups powdered sugar
1 egg
2 teaspoons grated lemon peel
1 teaspoon vanilla
3 cups all-purpose flour
½ teaspoon salt
1 recipe Royal Icing (page 61)

DECORATIONS
Assorted food colors, icings and candies

1 Beat butter and sugar in large bowl at high speed of electric mixer until fluffy. Add egg, lemon peel and vanilla; mix well. Combine flour and salt in medium bowl. Add to butter mixture; mix well.

2 Divide dough into 2 sections. Cover with plastic wrap. Refrigerate 3 hours or overnight.

3 Preheat oven to 375°F. Roll dough on floured surface to ⅛-inch thickness. Cut out cookies using Easter cookie cutters, such as eggs, bunnies and tulips. Place on ungreased cookie sheets.

4 Bake 8 to 12 minutes or just until edges are very lightly browned. Remove to wire racks; cool completely. Prepare Royal Icing. Decorate as desired. Let stand until icing is set.
Makes 4 dozen cookies

Festive Easter Cookies

Chocolate and Peanut Butter Hearts

What you need:

1 recipe Chocolate
    Cookie Dough
    (page 61)
½ cup creamy peanut
    butter
½ cup shortening
1 cup sugar
1 egg
1 teaspoon vanilla
3 tablespoons milk
2 cups all-purpose flour
1 teaspoon baking
    powder
¼ teaspoon salt

1 Prepare Chocolate Cookie Dough. Divide dough in half; wrap in plastic wrap. Refrigerate about 2 hours or until firm.

2 Beat peanut butter, shortening and sugar at medium speed of electric mixer until fluffy. Add egg and vanilla; mix until well blended. Add milk; mix well.

3 Combine flour, baking powder and salt in medium bowl. Add flour mixture to peanut butter mixture; mix at low speed until well blended. Divide dough in half; wrap in plastic wrap. Refrigerate 1 to 2 hours or until firm.

4 Preheat oven to 350°F. Grease cookie sheets. Roll ½ of peanut butter dough on floured waxed paper to ⅛-inch thickness. Cut out cookies using 3-inch heart-shaped cookie cutter. Place on prepared cookie sheets.

5 Use smaller heart-shaped cookie cutter to remove small section from center of heart; set smaller cutouts aside.

6 Repeat with chocolate dough. Place small hearts into opposite dough according to photo; press lightly.

7 Bake 12 to 14 minutes or until edges are lightly browned. Remove to wire racks; cool completely.
Makes 4 dozen cookies

Chocolate and Peanut Butter Hearts

Angels

What you need:

**1 recipe Butter Cookie
Dough (page 61)
1 egg, lightly beaten**

DECORATIONS
**Small pretzels, white
frosting, toasted
coconut, glitter dust
and assorted small
decors**

1 Prepare Butter Cookie
Dough. Refrigerate about
6 hours or until firm.

2 Preheat oven to 350°F.
Grease cookie sheets. Roll
dough on floured surface to
¼-inch thickness.

3 Cut out 12 (4-inch)
triangles according to
diagram. Reroll scraps to
¼-inch thickness. Cut out
12 (1½-inch) circles according
to diagram.

4 Place triangles on prepared
cookie sheets. Brush tops
with beaten egg. Attach circle,
pressing gently.

5 Bake 8 to 10 minutes or
just until edges begin to
brown. Remove to wire racks;
cool completely.

6 Attach pretzels to back of
each cookie for wings using
frosting as "glue". Let dry
30 minutes. Pipe frosting around
hairline of each angel; sprinkle
with coconut and glitter dust.

7 Pipe frosting on body of
cookie to resemble arms
and gown. Decorate faces as
desired. Let stand 1 hour or
until dry.

Makes 1 dozen cookies

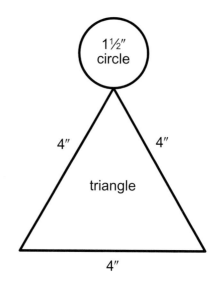

Christmas Tree Platter

What you need:

1 recipe Christmas
  Ornament Cookie
  Dough (page 62)
2 cups sifted powdered
  sugar
2 tablespoons milk or
  lemon juice

DECORATIONS

Assorted food colors,
  colored sugars and
  assorted small
  decors

1 Preheat oven to 350°F. Prepare Christmas Ornament Cookie Dough. Divide dough in half. Reserve 1 half; refrigerate remaining dough. Roll reserved half of dough to ⅛-inch thickness.

2 Cut out tree shapes with cookie cutters. Place on ungreased cookie sheets.

3 Bake 10 to 12 minutes or until edges are lightly browned. Remove to wire racks; cool completely.

4 Repeat with remaining half of dough. Reroll scraps; cut into small circles for ornaments, squares and rectangles for gift boxes and tree trunks.

5 Bake 8 to 12 minutes, depending on size of cookies.

6 Mix sugar and milk for icing. Tint most of icing green and a smaller amount red or other colors for ornaments and boxes. Spread green icing on trees. Sprinkle ornaments and boxes with colored sugars or decorate as desired.

7 Arrange cookies on flat platter to resemble tree as shown in photo.
Makes about 1 dozen cookies

Tip

Use this beautiful Christmas Tree Platter cookie as your centerpiece for this holiday's family dinner. It's sure to receive lots of "oohs" and "ahs"!

Christmas Tree Platter

Snowmen

What you need:

**1 package (20 ounces)
refrigerated
chocolate chip
cookie dough
1½ cups sifted powdered
sugar
2 tablespoons milk**

DECORATIONS

**Candy corn, gum
drops, chocolate
chips, licorice and
other assorted small
candies**

1 Preheat oven to 375°F.

2 Cut dough into 12 equal
sections. Divide each
section into 3 balls: large,
medium and small for each
snowman.

3 For each snowman, place
3 balls in a row, ¼ inch
apart, on ungreased cookie
sheet. Repeat with remaining
dough.

4 Bake 10 to 12 minutes or
until edges are very lightly
browned.

5 Cool 4 minutes on cookie
sheets. Remove to wire
racks; cool completely.

6 Mix powdered sugar and
milk in medium bowl until
smooth. Pour over cookies. Let
cookies stand 20 minutes or
until set.

7 Decorate to create faces,
hats and arms with
assorted candies.
Makes 1 dozen cookies

*Create your own winter
wonderland in the warmth of your
holiday kitchen. Then, let the kids
add their own touch with their
creative decorating.*

Yield and baking times have not been included for these cookies. For best results, prepare and bake as directed in individual recipes.

Gingerbread Cookie Dough

What you need:

½ **cup shortening**
⅓ **cup packed light brown sugar**
¼ **cup dark molasses**
1 **egg white**
½ **teaspoon vanilla**
1½ **cups all-purpose flour**
1 **teaspoon ground cinnamon**
½ **teaspoon baking soda**
½ **teaspoon salt**
½ **teaspoon ground ginger**
¼ **teaspoon baking powder**

1 Beat shortening, brown sugar, molasses, egg white and vanilla in large bowl at high speed of electric mixer until smooth.

2 Combine flour, cinnamon, baking soda, salt, ginger and baking powder in small bowl. Add to shortening mixture; mix well. Cover; refrigerate about 8 hours or until firm.

Butter Cookie Dough

What you need:

¾ cup butter or
     margarine, softened
¼ cup granulated sugar
¼ cup packed light
     brown sugar
1 egg yolk
1¾ cups all-purpose flour
¾ teaspoon baking
     powder
⅛ teaspoon salt

1 Combine butter, granulated sugar, brown sugar and egg yolk in medium bowl. Add flour, baking powder and salt; mix well.

2 Cover; refrigerate about 4 hours or until firm.

Royal Icing

What you need:

1 egg white, at room
     temperature
2 to 2½ cups sifted
     powdered sugar
½ teaspoon almond
     extract

1 Beat egg white in small bowl at high speed of electric mixer until foamy.

2 Gradually add 2 cups powdered sugar and almond extract. Beat at low speed until moistened. Increase mixer speed to high and beat until icing is stiff.

Chocolate Cookie Dough

What you need:

1 cup butter or
     margarine, softened
1 cup sugar
1 egg
1 teaspoon vanilla
2 ounces semisweet
     chocolate, melted
2¼ cups all-purpose flour
1 teaspoon baking
     powder
¼ teaspoon salt

1 Beat butter and sugar in large bowl at high speed of electric mixer until fluffy. Beat in egg and vanilla. Add melted chocolate; mix well.

2 Add flour, baking powder and salt; mix well. Cover; refrigerate about 2 hours or until firm.

Lemonade Royal Icing

What you need:

3¾ cups sifted powdered
     sugar
3 tablespoons meringue
     powder
6 tablespoons frozen
     lemonade
     concentrate, thawed

Beat all ingredients in large bowl at high speed of electric mixer until smooth.

Christmas Ornament Cookie Dough

What you need:

2¼ cups all-purpose flour
¼ teaspoon salt
1 cup sugar
¾ cup butter or
    margarine, softened
1 egg
1 teaspoon vanilla
1 teaspoon almond
    extract

1 Combine flour and salt in medium bowl.

2 Beat sugar and butter in large bowl at medium speed of electric mixer until fluffy. Beat in egg, vanilla and almond extract. Gradually add flour mixture. Beat at low speed until well blended.

3 Form dough into 2 discs; wrap in plastic wrap and refrigerate 30 minutes or until firm.

Cookie Glaze

What you need:

4 cups powdered sugar
4 to 6 tablespoons milk

Combine powdered sugar and enough milk, 1 tablespoon at a time, to make a medium-thick pourable glaze.

Gingerbread Construction Dough

What you need:

5¼ cups all-purpose flour
1 tablespoon ground
    ginger
2 teaspoons baking
    soda
1½ teaspoons ground
    allspice
1 teaspoon salt
2 cups packed dark
    brown sugar
1 cup butter or
    margarine, softened
¾ cup dark corn syrup
2 eggs

1 Combine flour, ginger, baking soda, allspice and salt in medium bowl.

2 Beat brown sugar and butter in large bowl at medium speed of electric mixer until fluffy. Beat in corn syrup and eggs. Gradually add flour mixture. Beat at low speed until well blended. Cover; refrigerate about 2 hours or until firm.

METRIC CONVERSION CHART

VOLUME MEASUREMENTS (dry)

⅛ teaspoon = 0.5 mL

¼ teaspoon = 1 mL

½ teaspoon = 2 mL

¾ teaspoon = 4 mL

1 teaspoon = 5 mL

1 tablespoon = 15 mL

2 tablespoons = 30 mL

¼ cup = 60 mL

⅓ cup = 75 mL

½ cup = 125 mL

⅔ cup = 150 mL

¾ cup = 175 mL

1 cup = 250 mL

2 cups = 1 pint = 500 mL

3 cups = 750 mL

4 cups = 1 quart = 1 L

VOLUME MEASUREMENTS (fluid)

1 fluid ounce (2 tablespoons) = 30 mL

4 fluid ounces (½ cup) = 125 mL

8 fluid ounces (1 cup) = 250 mL

12 fluid ounces (1½ cups) = 375 mL

16 fluid ounces (2 cups) = 500 mL

WEIGHTS (mass)

½ ounce = 15 g

1 ounce = 30 g

3 ounces = 90 g

4 ounces = 120 g

8 ounces = 225 g

10 ounces = 285 g

12 ounces = 360 g

16 ounces = 1 pound = 450 g

DIMENSIONS

1/16 inch = 2 mm

⅛ inch = 3 mm

¼ inch = 6 mm

½ inch = 1.5 cm

¾ inch = 2 cm

1 inch = 2.5 cm

OVEN TEMPERATURES

250°F = 120°C

275°F = 140°C

300°F = 150°C

325°F = 160°C

350°F = 180°C

375°F = 190°C

400°F = 200°C

425°F = 220°C

450°F = 230°C

BAKING PAN SIZES

Utensil	Size in Inches/ Quarts	Metric Volume	Size in Centimeters
Baking or Cake Pan (square or rectangular)	8 × 8 × 2	2 L	20 × 20 × 5
	9 × 9 × 2	2.5 L	23 × 23 × 5
	12 × 8 × 2	3 L	30 × 20 × 5
	13 × 9 × 2	3.5 L	33 × 23 × 5
Loaf Pan	8 × 4 × 3	1.5 L	20 × 10 × 7
	9 × 5 × 3	2 L	23 × 13 × 7
Round Layer Cake Pan	8 × 1½	1.2 L	20 × 4
	9 × 1½	1.5 L	23 × 4
Pie Plate	8 × 1¼	750 mL	20 × 3
	9 × 1¼	1 L	23 × 3
Baking Dish or Casserole	1 quart	1 L	—
	1½ quart	1.5 L	—
	2 quart	2 L	—